THE MAD SCIENTIST'S NOTEBOOK

THE MAD SCIENTIST'S NOTEBOOK

Warning: Dangerously Wacky Experiments Inside

Elizabeth Snoke Harris & Rain Newcomb

Illustrated by Ian Nagy

LARK BOOKS

A Division of Sterling Publishing Co., Inc.
New York / London

Creative Director
CELIA NARANJO
Cover Art
IAN NAGY

Editorial Assistant: Rose McLarney
Art Assistant: Bradley Norris

Library of Congress Cataloging-in-Publication Data

Harris, Elizabeth Snoke, 1973-
 The mad scientist's notebook : warning! dangerously wacky experiments inside / by Elizabeth Snoke Harris and Rain Newcomb ; illustrated by Ian Nagy. -- 1st ed.
   p. cm.
 Includes index.
 ISBN-13: 978-1-60059-009-2 (hc-plc with jacket : alk. paper)
 ISBN-10: 1-60059-009-8 (hc-plc with jacket : alk. paper)
 1. Science--Experiments--Juvenile literature. I. Newcomb, Rain.
II. Nagy, Ian. III. Title.
 Q164.H268 2008
 507.8--dc22

                            2007038893

10 9 8 7 6 5 4 3 2 1

First Edition

Published by Lark Books, A Division of
Sterling Publishing Co., Inc.
387 Park Avenue South, New York, NY 10016

Distributed in Canada by Sterling Publishing,
c/o Canadian Manda Group, 165 Dufferin Street
Toronto, Ontario, Canada M6K 3H6

Distributed in the United Kingdom by GMC Distribution Services,
Castle Place, 166 High Street, Lewes, East Sussex, England BN7 1XU
Distributed in Australia by Capricorn Link (Australia) Pty Ltd.,
P.O. Box 704, Windsor, NSW 2756 Australia

If you have questions or comments about this book, please contact:

Lark Books
67 Broadway
Asheville, NC 28801
828-253-0467

Manufactured in China

ISBN 13: 978-1-60059-009-2
ISBN 10: 1-60059-009-8

For information about custom editions, special sales, premium and corporate purchases, please contact Sterling Special Sales Department at 800-805-5489 or specialsales@sterlingpub.com.

CONTENTS

WELCOME TO THE LAB

This notebook is the result of 42 years of exhaustive research, 15 different assistants, and seven laboratories. The journey has been perilous, but no risk is too great when you're in pursuit of science! (Besides, that's what lab assistants are for.)

Four of my assistants were eaten by experiments gone wrong, three exploded, six were transformed with varying degrees of success, and two were actually spies from the Research and Development arm of Mad Scientists, Inc. For legal reasons, I'm not allowed to talk about what happened to the laboratories.

Each experiment in my notebook contains a list of items you need and step-by-step instructions to duplicate it. The things you need may require an occasional trip to the store, but you probably already have most of them in your house.

Read through the entire experiment before you begin. I made the mistake of not doing this once and accidentally sunk my island laboratory (after I had set it on fire).

At the end of each experiment, there is a brief explanation of the scientific principles at work. Plus a few notes about how I plan to twist the laws of nature to serve my own manic machinations. My favorite words appear in RED—you'll find their definitions in the glossary on page 78.

It is my fondest hope that the information within this notebook will assist budding Mad Scientists. So develop outrageous experiments, hatch wild plots, and push the boundaries of science farther than they've ever been pushed before!

COIN OPERATED LIGHT

Ever since my lab assistant turned into a giant chicken, I've been having a terrible time paying the bills on time. So here's what I'll do the next time the lights go out.

PROCURE THESE ITEMS

- Paper towel
- Scissors
- Lemon juice
- 6 pennies
- 6 dimes or nickels
- 2 pieces of insulated copper wire with each end stripped
- LED light with exposed wires*
- Tape

   *You can find these little lights at your favorite electronics supply store.

DO EXACTLY WHAT IT SAYS HERE

1. Cut the paper towel into 1-inch (2.5 cm) squares with the scissors. (Do this BEFORE the power is turned off.) You'll need 11 squares of paper towel.

2. Soak the squares in lemon juice.

3. Stack the coins, alternating pennies with the dimes or nickels. Slip a square of paper towel between each one. You should have a coin on each end of the stack.

4. Lick the index finger of each hand. Hold the pile between your index fingers. Shocking!

5. Wrap the stripped end of the first piece of copper wire around one of the stiff wire prongs coming out of the LED light. Wrap the stripped end of the other piece of wire around the other prong.

6. Make a loop in the free end of each copper wire. Tape each loop flat against one end of the pile of coins.

ZAP!

You felt a small shock or tingle when you touched the stack of coins with wet fingers because you made a VOLTAIC PILE, the primitive ancestor of today's battery.

The metal coins have a loose hold on their ELECTRONS. When there's a CONDUCTOR in between the metals, such as the lemon juice, the metals pass their electrons back and forth. This creates an electric current.

You could use any ACID to do this, but lemon juice won't eat away the coins (destroying your battery) or your fingers (destroying your ability to conduct further experiments). The little LED light will stay on for about two hours, just long enough for me to finish my notes and make another one!

FRUIT POWER!

When I can't find any spare change, I go straight for the lemon.

PROCURE THESE ITEMS

- 4 nails or paper clips, straightened
- At least 4 lemons (or other fruit)
- Wire cutters
- Heavy copper wire*
- LED light with exposed wires**

  *If you're using insulated copper wire, strip the ends of each piece you use, as shown in the illustration.

  **You can find these little lights at your favorite electronics supply store.

DO EXACTLY WHAT IT SAYS HERE

1. Stick a nail into the top of the first lemon. Cut a 5-inch (12.7 cm) piece of copper wire and stick one end into the top of the same lemon. The nail and the wire should be close together, but not touching.

2. Repeat step 1 with each lemon.

3. Connect the lemons in a series by wrapping the end of a piece of copper wire from one lemon around the nail in the next lemon. Leave the nail in one lemon and the copper wire in another lemon free.

4. Cut one long piece of copper wire. Wrap one end around the free nail. Wrap the other end of the wire around one of the prongs sticking out from the bottom of the LED.

5. Wrap the end of the copper wire sticking out of the last lemon around the other prong sticking out from the bottom of the LED.

ZAP!

This experiment creates electricity the same way the VOLTAIC PILE does. The ELECTRONS in the nail and copper wire travel back and forth through the lemon juice CONDUCTOR, generating an electrical current.

Each lemon in the sequence is called a CELL, because it has the nail and copper wire sticking into it. The nail is the negative terminal and the copper wire is the positive terminal. The electricity flows from the negative terminal to the positive terminal.

Each lemon supplies about ¼ to ⅓ volt of electricity, which is why you have to connect several to power the LED light. The more cells you have connected to each other, the more electricity can be produced. The batteries you buy at the store contain several cells inside the metal casing.

Now I just need to figure out how to grow a lemon large enough to power my electric car!

TOWING GLACIERS

With the right equipment, you can pick up a piece of ice without touching it!

PROCURE THESE ITEMS

- Glass
- Water
- Ice cubes
- Plate
- Cotton string
- Salt

DO EXACTLY WHAT IT SAYS HERE

1. Fill the glass with water. Set it aside for the moment.

2. Put the ice cubes on the plate.

3. Dip the end of the string in the glass of water.

4. Lay the wet end of the string on top of an ice cube.

5. Sprinkle some salt over the end of the string and the ice cube.

6. Wait 15 or 20 seconds. Then pick up the string—the ice cube will come with it.

THE STICKING POINT

You froze the string to the top of the ice cube, which is what let you pick it up. Ice melts above 32°F (0°C)—and unless you're a penguin, your home is much warmer than that. The ice cube started to melt as soon as it was taken out of the freezer.

Adding salt lowers the ice's MELTING POINT. (The melting point is the temperature at which a solid turns into a liquid.) Normally, a little bit of the melted water on top of the ice cube would refreeze (because the ice cube is still cold). But the salt makes the ice melt faster than it freezes.

When you put the string on top of the ice cube, the ice cube absorbs heat from the wet string and from the air. As the heat gets sucked out of the water in the string, the water and the string freeze to the ice cube.

I plan on using this little trick to hook a bunch of glaciers together. Then I'll put a giant fan on the first glacier and sail my glacier chain around the world. And when I come across countries that won't pay attention to global warming, I'll crash my glaciers into their coastlines! What good is being a Mad Scientist if you can't save the polar bears?

MAGNETIC ATTRACTION

This experiment combines three of the most awesome powers in the universe: magnets, electricity, and my brain!

PROCURE THESE ITEMS

- Medium gauge copper wire
- Wire cutter
- Screwdriver
- Tape
- Battery (AA, C, or D)
- Paper clips

DO EXACTLY WHAT IT SAYS HERE

1. Cut a 12-inch (30.5 cm) long piece of wire. Starting with the middle of the wire, wrap it around the screwdriver 10 times. Leave at least 3 inches (7.6 cm) of wire hanging down at each end.

2. Tape one end of the wire to the negative terminal on the battery. (It's marked with a "−" sign.) Make sure the metal parts are touching.

3. Hold the screwdriver by the handle. With the other hand, touch the free end of the wire to the positive terminal on the battery. (It's marked with a "+" sign.) You can tape the wire in place if you want.

4. Pass the screwdriver over the paper clips.

5. Disconnect the wire from the battery and wrap twice as much wire around the screwdriver. Then repeat steps 2 through 4. How much more powerful is the electromagnet?

THE SECRET OF MAGNETISM

ELECTRONS are subatomic particles that spin like crazy around the NUCLEUS of an atom. When electrons spin or move in the same direction, they create a magnetic force field that pulls other electrons along with them.

When you connect a piece of wire to the ends of a battery, electrons flow through the wire, creating a magnetic field. If you wrap the wire around a screwdriver, the magnetic field in the wire makes the electrons in the screwdriver spin in such a way that they create a magnetic field, too. As you coil more wire around the screwdriver, the magnetic field grows stronger and stronger.

I could make an electromagnet strong enough to pull the Moon out of its orbit! My ransom note is ready. Now, all I need is 2,319 miles (3,732 km) of copper wire, a screwdriver the length of Texas, and a really big battery.

MEMO
To: Leaders of the World
From: The Mad Scientist
Re: The Extinction of Life as We Know It

I have created an electromagnet strong enough to crash the Moon into the Earth. I will begin the destruction sequence unless the following demands are met:

1. 24 gazillion dollars, in nickels, dimes, and pennies
2. A quiet, deserted island for my secret laboratory with a year-round temperature 82°F (27.8°C) and a cool southwest breeze
3. A ½ gallon (1.98 ℓ) of chocolate chip cookie dough ice cream

You have until midnight to comply.

DIS-SOLVING THE PROBLEM

Some days, my biggest challenge is figuring out what to do with all the packing peanuts that came with the Death Ray I ordered from the back of my Hi-Jinx Cereal box.

PROCURE THESE ITEMS

- Cornstarch packing peanuts
- Glass cup, jar, or bowl
- Water
- Spoon

DO EXACTLY WHAT IT SAYS HERE

1. Put a packing peanut in the glass cup, jar, or bowl. (It doesn't really matter which one you use. It's just best if it's see-through so you can watch the melting happen.)

2. Pour a little bit of water onto the peanut. Watch it melt. Can you hear it scream?

3. Stuff the cup with packing peanuts. Slowly pour water over the peanuts. Watch the peanuts dissolve.

4. When the peanuts are completely dissolved, play with the liquid. Stir it with the spoon. Now hit it hard with the spoon. Is it really a liquid at all? If you're really hungry, you can eat the leftover peanuts. (They won't taste very good though.)

WHEN WORLDS COLLOID

Actually, the packing peanuts didn't really DISSOLVE at all. They just broke into little tiny pieces—pieces too small to see with the naked eye. These pieces are very light. They float on top of the water instead of dissolving or sinking to the bottom.

When the little bits of peanut float on top of the water, they stick together. If you hit the liquid hard, the spoon will hit a wall of teeny peanut bits. But if you slowly touch the liquid with the spoon, the peanut bits will ooze out of the way and your spoon will sink into it. This type of substance is called a COLLOID.

The applications of this principle are endless—all I need to do is convince a few banks to build their vaults out of packing peanuts. Then I can waltz in with a bottle of water, melt a hole in the wall, and waltz right back out. I'm sure this little advertisement will do the trick.

THE NEW WATER REMOVAL SYSTEM

This is just a little something I cooked up when the lab flooded. It got rid of the water fast! (But only temporarily.)

PROCURE THESE ITEMS

- Votive candle
- Aluminum pie plate
- Matches
- Water
- Jar (larger than the candle)

DO EXACTLY WHAT IT SAYS HERE

1. Put the candle in the pie pan. Light it.

2. Carefully pour water into the pie pan. Pour just enough water to float the candle.

3. Quickly invert the jar over the candle.

4. Watch!

THE ALL-WET EXPLANATION

As the candle burns, it heats up the air above it. When the air heats, it expands. (Did you hear the jar rattle against the plate? That was the hot air escaping because there wasn't enough room in the jar for it.)

The inside of the jar got a little dewy because the hot gases CONDENSED (turned back into a liquid) when they touched the cool surface of the glass.

When the candle burned up all the oxygen inside the jar, the candle went out. The hot air in the jar cooled quickly. When it cooled, it became DENSER, taking up less room. Something had to fill the space the air vacated, so the water was sucked into the glass!

This experiment is good for when you want to do a little fundraising from ancient shipwrecks, or if you just want to ruin a whole bunch of people's beach vacations. You do need an awfully big candle though.

ELECTRORHEOLOGICAL FLUID

I've done this experiment so many times, my hair permanently stands on end.

PROCURE THESE ITEMS

- Measuring cup
- Vegetable oil
- Cup
- Cornstarch
- Spoon
- Balloon
- Your head
- Bowl

DO EXACTLY WHAT IT SAYS HERE

1. Pour ½ cup (118 ml) of vegetable oil into the cup. Stir in about ¾ cup (177 ml) of cornstarch with the spoon. Keep adding cornstarch until you have a mixture about the consistency of gravy. It should pour, but should not be runny.

2. Blow up the balloon and tie a knot in the end. Rub it on your head until all of your hair stands on end.

3. Hold the balloon in one hand. With the other hand, slowly pour the mixture from the cup into the bowl. Bring the balloon close to the thin stream of fluid.

4. Don't freak out. The fluid will bend and stop moving when it enters the electrical field from the balloon. (Feel free to freak other people out with this experiment though.)

NOTE: When you're tired of playing with your electrorheological fluid, you can pour it down the drain.

AN EXPLANATION (SORT OF)

Cornstarch is electrically active, which means it reacts to an electric field. When you mix the cornstarch into the vegetable oil, it doesn't DISSOLVE. It gets suspended, which means it sort of floats in the liquid (making a COLLOID). The vegetable oil holds the cornstarch, so the cornstarch will pour and flow like a liquid.

When the cornstarch colloid is exposed to an electrical field, such as the balloon you charged up with your hair, it reacts. The VISCOSITY (how much the liquid flows) of the colloid changes and it appears to become solid. Any fluid that reacts to an electrical field is called ELECTRORHEOLOGICAL.

Nobody, including me, is entirely sure how this works. Basically, each cornstarch particle is made up of millions of atoms. A little tiny bit of each atom reacts to the electrical field. This little tiny bit reacts the same way in every atom in every particle of cornstarch. All the little tiny bits link together and form a new bond, turning the liquid into something that acts like a solid. The trick is that you have to have just the right amount of electricity to make this experiment work.

Electrorheological fluid is the secret component in all of my robots. Of course, every time the electricity goes out, I have to run around rubbing balloons on my head to get the robots to work again.

A-MAZE-ING POTATO

I stayed up late last night wondering if I'm smarter than a potato. This is the experiment I designed to figure it out.

PROCURE THESE ITEMS

- Sprouting potato
- Shoebox
- Scissors
- Cardboard
- Tape

DO EXACTLY WHAT IT SAYS HERE

1. To construct a maze for the potato, start by cutting a ½-inch (1.3 cm) hole in one end of the shoebox. This is the end of the maze.

2. Use the cardboard, scissors, and tape to make a maze inside the shoebox. Make sure each "wall" has some way for the potato to wiggle through, such as a hole or a gap. Don't make the maze too difficult for the potato—after all, it's just a potato.

3. Put the potato in the shoebox, opposite the hole you made in step 1. Put the lid on.

4. Place the shoebox in a sunny place. Make sure sunlight shines through the hole in the box.

5. Check on the potato every three or four days. Be careful when taking the lid off—domesticated potatoes can become feral if left alone in the dark for too long.

6. Time how long it takes the potato sprouts to find the light. If the potato isn't doing well, take pity on it and remove a few walls!

THE SECRET OF THE SOLAR SPUD

The potato sprout eventually made its way to the light. Plants make their food out of sunlight by a process called PHOTOSYNTHESIS. So, in order for the potato to eat, it had to find the sun.

Special pigments in the potato (called phytochromes) react to the sunlight, causing the plant to bend and grow toward the light. The potato can sense where the light is shining into the shoebox through the little hole and grows toward it.

Potatoes and other plants that orient themselves to the sun are called HELIOTROPIC.

Now I know to move away from the light, particularly early in the morning. By shoving my head under piles of pillows and blankets, I can seal out all solar interference. Then I can sleep for a few more hours. In my humble opinion, this makes me much, much smarter than your average potato.

INERTIA HAT

I wear this hat to The Mad Scientist Convention every year.
They love me there.

PROCURE THESE ITEMS

- Wire cutters
- Wire coat hanger
- Modeling clay or play dough

DO EXACTLY WHAT IT SAYS HERE

1. Use the wire cutters to cut the hook part off the coat hanger. Get rid of the hook. Straighten out the remaining wire.

2. Bend the wire into the shape shown in my snapshot. Start by making the wire into a V. Make sure the point of the V is in the exact center of the wire. Then bend the ends of the V down to make an M shape. The bottom ends of the M should be about 6 inches (15.2 cm) lower than the point of the V.

3. Use the modeling clay to make two balls, each about the size of a plum. The balls should be the same size. Stick one on each end of the wire.

4. Balance the point of the wire on the top of your head. Turn your head to the left, then to the right. The Inertia Hat won't move. Now hold your head still. Put one finger on each ball and push the Inertia Hat so it spins around your head.

EUREKA!

The Inertia Hat takes advantage of the laws of INERTIA (hence the name). Inertia is the tendency of an object at rest to stay at rest and an object in motion to stay in motion (unless it is acted upon by an outside force).

When the Inertia Hat is still (at rest) and You turn Your head, the hat stays still (at rest). When the Inertia Hat is moving, and You're staying still, the hat keeps moving.

Unfortunately, the Inertia Hat will eventually stop moving. That's because there's FRICTION between the Inertia Hat and the air, and friction between the point of the hat and the top of Your head. The Inertia Hat has to use a tiny bit of energy to overcome the friction every time it moves. Eventually, this makes the Inertia Hat run out of energy.

In a VACUUM, like in outer space, this wouldn't be a problem. That's because a vacuum has no matter, which means there's no air (or anything else) to create friction.

So if I want my Inertia Hat to keep moving forever, I just need to suck all of the air out of the atmosphere to create a complete vacuum. Now there's an idea!

MY ALL-TIME FAVORITE EXCUSE

To Whom It May Concern:

The Mad Scientist will not be coming into the lab today. He is unable to overcome the awesome force of inertia, and therefore must remain in bed for the rest of the day.

GRAVITY GOT YOU DOWN?

Gravity, the force that keeps me in my bed at night, is a real drag sometimes—particularly when I drop my toast on the ground. Here's an experiment I cooked up in an attempt to reverse gravity.

PROCURE THESE ITEMS

- Book, at least 1 inch (2.5 cm) thick
- 2 brand-new pencils
- Ping-Pong ball

DO EXACTLY WHAT IT SAYS HERE

1. Lay the book on the table. Rest the erasers of both pencils on the spine of the book. They should be about 1½ inches (3.8 cm) apart.

2. Put the sharpened ends of the pencils together on the table. (You don't have to sharpen the pencils though.) You now have a V-shaped ramp.

3. Place the Ping-Pong ball in between the pencils at the top of the ramp. Let it go. What happens?

4. To restore gravity to its proper alignment, reverse the V. (Make the wide part of the ramp on the ground and the point on the book.)

FULL DISCLOSURE

This experiment doesn't actually change GRAVITY. (Boo hoo.) It just takes advantage of the Ping-Pong ball's CENTER OF GRAVITY. The center of gravity is the point around which all of the object's weight is balanced. For a symmetrical object, such as the Ping-Pong ball, the center of gravity is the point in the very middle.

When the Ping-Pong ball rolls along the ramp, gravity doesn't change, but the area on the ramp supporting the ball does. When the ramp is narrow, the ball sits up high. As the ramp widens, the ball sits down lower and is actually being held up by its sides. This means that the ball's center is actually lower (relative to the ramp).

Try the experiment again, but this time look at the ball relative to the tabletop. It's actually moving down while it appears to be moving up. This is an optical illusion!

So all I have to do is figure out how to change my center of gravity by redistributing my weight. Then I too can defy gravity! (Sort of.)

WASHING SODA ASTEROIDS

Until I get the Time Machine back from the mechanics, I can't do any time traveling. So I cooked up this little experiment to figure out if a giant asteroid crashed into the Earth and made the dinosaurs extinct.

PROCURE THESE ITEMS

- Paper cup
- Hot water
- Washing soda*
- Spoon
- Paper plate

  *You can find this on the laundry aisle of the grocery store.

DO EXACTLY WHAT IT SAYS HERE

1. Fill the cup half full with hot water. (The hot water from your faucet will be warm enough. You don't need to heat it up any more than that.)

2. Pour some washing soda into the water. Stir it with the spoon while you pour. Keep adding washing soda until it stops dissolving. (You'll know the washing soda isn't dissolving anymore when you can still see it in the cup.)

3. Leave the cup alone for a few hours. Then come back and look at it. You should see crystals forming on the sides and bottom of the cup.

4. Pour the crystals from the cup onto a paper plate. Put the plate in a warm, sunny place. Go away for 24 hours. Then come back and see how the crystals have grown.

THE SOLUTION'S A SOLUTION

When you mix the water and washing soda together, the solids (washing soda) DISSOLVE in the liquid (water), forming a SOLUTION. In a solution, the solids are called the SOLUTE and the liquid is called the SOLVENT. Eventually, the solvent can't hold any more solute. At this point, you can see tiny grains of solute floating around in the cup. You now have a SATURATED SOLUTION.

As the solvent EVAPORATES, it has to let go of the solute. The solute sticks together on the cup and forms crystals. The type of solute that you use will determine the shape the crystals make. Washing soda makes crystals that look just like tiny asteroids.

My plan is to crash a really gigantic washing soda asteroid into my terrarium to see if that's what made the dinosaurs extinct. I wonder if these little plastic dinosaur toys will be a good stand-in for the real thing.

DNA EXTRACTION

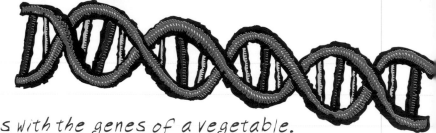

I'm trying to splice my genes with the genes of a vegetable.
Then I won't have to eat them anymore!

PROCURE THESE ITEMS

- Ethyl alcohol (95 percent ethanol)
- Refrigerator
- Spinach*
- Knife
- Cutting board
- Blender or food processor
- Extraction solution (see sticky note)
- Measuring spoons
- Large bowl of ice water
- Strainer
- Clean spaghetti-sauce or pickle jar
- Pantyhose
- Large test tube with stopper
  (or baby-food jar with lid)
- Round toothpicks

*If you've banned spinach from the premises of your kitchen, you can use kiwis, onions, or strawberries.

DO EXACTLY WHAT IT SAYS HERE

1. Chill the ethyl alcohol by putting it in the fridge for at least two hours.

2. Cut a handful of spinach into 1-inch (2.5 cm) pieces.

3. Put the spinach in the blender. Add 4 tablespoons (60 ml) of extraction solution. Blend the mixture for about five minutes.

4. Put the container from the blender in the bowl of ice water to cool the mixture. Leave it in there for one minute. Then blend the mixture for five minutes. Do this five times.

5. Place the strainer over the large jar. Stretch the pantyhose over the strainer. Filter the mixture through the pantyhose and strainer.

EXTRACTION SOLUTION

This recipe will make enough solution to perform five extractions.

PROCURE THESE ITEMS

- ½ cup (118 ml) shampoo*
- 1 tablespoon (20 g) table salt
- Container
- Water
- Tablespoon

  *Do not use shampoo with conditioner or baby shampoo.

MAKE THE EXTRACTION SOLUTION

1. Mix the shampoo and table salt together in the container.
2. Add water to make a final volume of 4 ¼ cups (1 ℓ).
3. Stir slowly to dissolve the salt. Try to avoid making the mixture foam.

6. Pour 1 tablespoon (15 ml) of the filtered solution into the test tube.
7. Being careful not to shake the test tube, add 1 tablespoon (15 ml) of cold ethyl alcohol to the test tube. Pour it down the side of the tube so it will float on top of the filtered solution.
8. Look closely at the test tube. The spinach DNA is floating at the very top.
9. Gently twirl the DNA around a toothpick to remove it.

HOW THE EXTRACTION PROCESS WORKS

DNA, the long MOLECULE found in the NUCLEUS at the center of each CELL, contains genetic information that tells the cells what they're going to become. :ry living thing has DNA.

In order to extract the DNA, first you open the cell wall with the blender. Then the soap in the extraction solution destroys the rest of the cell walls and eats up the MEMBRANE of the nucleus, so the DNA can escape. The salt makes the proteins and carbohydrates that make up the rest of the cell sink to the bottom. The DNA floats on top.

Cooling the mixture protects the DNA from ENZYMES in the cell that can destroy the DNA. (These enzymes normally protect the cell from outside DNA, like viruses.) Adding cool ethanol to the mixture increases the amount of DNA you can separate from the rest of the cell walls.

The process of grafting vegetable DNA to my DNA has hit a snag, so I've put this experiment on a back Bunsen burner. I think I'll raise an army of zombie vegetables instead.

NAKED EGGS

How would you like your eggs? Bouncy or transparent?

PROCURE THESE ITEMS

- Eggs
- Lasagna pan
- Vinegar
- Aluminum foil
- Refrigerator
- Big spoon

DO EGGS-ACTLY WHAT IT SAYS HERE

1. Put the eggs in the lasagna pan. Arrange them so they aren't touching each other.

2. Pour the vinegar into the pan. Use enough vinegar to completely cover the eggs.

3. Use the aluminum foil to cover the pan. Put it in the fridge.

4. Go away for **24** hours. Now would be a good time to finish that essay on 14th-century inventors.

5. Take the pan out of the fridge. Use the big spoon to remove the eggs very carefully. Pour out the vinegar.

6. Gently squeeze the eggs with your hand. (Do this outside or over the sink if you have a particularly strong grip.) Hold an egg 3 inches (7.6 cm) above the sink (or sidewalk). Then let it go. How high can you drop an egg from before it breaks instead of bounces?

7. Put the eggs back in the pan. Cover them with vinegar again. Then replace the aluminum foil and put the pan back in the fridge.

8. Do something else for 24 hours.

9. Come back, take the pan out of the fridge, and remove the eggs. This time, the eggs are completely naked and you'll be able to see inside of them. If you don't want egg on your face, your hands, your clothes, or anywhere else, don't squeeze or bounce the egg this time.

NOTE: Don't eat these eggs, and wash your hands with hot soapy water after handling them. Nobody wants to bleed from the ears!

THE SCIENCE EGGS-PLAINED

The shell of an egg is made of calcium carbonate, a hard substance that protects the inside of the egg. The vinegar reacts with the calcium carbonate in the egg's shell, turning it into carbon dioxide and calcium acetate. The carbon dioxide is a GAS that escapes in little tiny bubbles, like the bubbles in soda. The calcium acetate is DISSOLVED by the water and the egg's shell disappears!

Without the hard shell, the eggs soak up the water in the vinegar, making them rubbery and bounceable. The amount of water inside each egg and the amount of water in the pan had to equal out. The vinegar in the pan is 95 percent water. That's a lot more watery than the inside of the egg. So the water in the pan oozed through the tiny, impossible-to-see spaces in the egg's MEMBRANE and into the egg, until there was the same amount of water inside the egg as in the pan. (This process is called OSMOSIS.)

Between the rubbery membrane and the extra water in the egg, the egg will bounce. For a little while. When you dissolve the entire shell, you can see right through the egg. It won't bounce anymore after that happens.

I developed this project for my first (and only) paying job. A farmer was having problems with her eggs breaking when the chickens sat on them. I came up with this nifty little solution. Unfortunately, the chickens just bounced out of their nests.

POSSESSED PASTA

Spaghetti is heavier than water, right? So it sinks when you put it in a bowl of water. Unless it's CRAZY water!

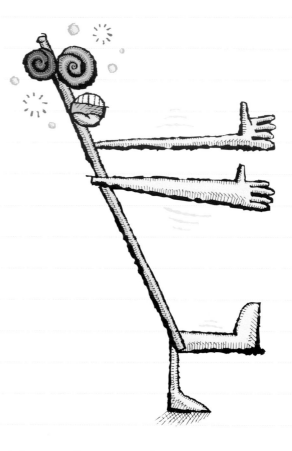

PROCURE THESE ITEMS

- Vermicelli noodle*
- Glass bowl
- Water
- Teaspoon
- Baking soda
- Vinegar
- Wooden spoon

   *Any pasta will work for this experiment, but the smaller and lighter it is, the better it will work.

DO EXACTLY WHAT IT SAYS HERE

1. Break a piece of vermicelli into 1-inch (2.5 cm) pieces. (Your fingers work better than a chainsaw for this.)

2. Fill the bowl two-thirds full with water.

3. Put 3 teaspoons (15 ml) of baking soda and 4 or 5 teaspoons (20 or 25 ml) of vinegar into the water. Stir the mixture with the wooden spoon.

4. Put the 1-inch (2.5 cm) pieces of vermicelli into the water. The pieces of vermicelli will rise to the surface and then sink to the bottom again.

5. Did anything happen? If not, repeat step 3, adding more baking soda and vinegar to the water.

THE NOT-SO-SUPERNATURAL EXPLANATION

There's not a poltergeist in the bowl. It's just chemistry! The acetic acid in the vinegar reacts with the baking soda, making carbon dioxide (a GAS). The carbon dioxide sticks to the pieces of vermicelli. Because the carbon dioxide gas is less DENSE than the water/vinegar mixture, the bubbles rise to the top, lifting the pieces of vermicelli with them. At the water's surface, the carbon dioxide bubbles let go and the vermicelli sinks to the bottom. Then the process starts all over again.

This experiment moves the vermicelli around in the bowl just like boiling water does. When water boils, bubbles move from the bottom of the pot to the top. The water at the top cools (but still not cool enough to touch!), sinks, heats up, and then rises again.

This fascinating scientific principle is called CONVECTION. Convection is one of the many ways heat travels. Convection happens in more places than a pot of boiling water. It's also happening in the atmosphere all the time. Warm air rises from the surface of the Earth, high into the atmosphere. There, it cools and sinks back to the surface.

Since this experiment works just like convection, I tried making dinner with it. MY pasta was crunchy and tasted kind of vinegary. This was not a good shortcut.

37

SINGING ROD

This is the instrument I play in my rock band.

PROCURE THESE ITEMS

- Metal rod, 3 to 6 feet (0.9 to 1.8 m) long
- Wax paper
- Both hands

DO EXACTLY WHAT IT SAYS HERE

1. Rub half of the rod with a piece of wax paper, coating it with wax.
    To make sure the rod is as waxy as possible, use both sides of the
    wax paper.

2. Balance the rod between your index fingers. Slowly move your fingers together. They'll meet in the middle of the rod.

3. Support the middle of the rod with one hand. (The rod should be balanced on your hand.) Use the index finger and thumb on your other hand to gently stroke the waxed side of the rod.

4. Do you hear a singing sound? Eureka! The more you rub the rod with your finger, the louder the sound will get.

WHAT'S THAT SOUND?

When you drag your finger across the waxed surface of the rod, your finger slips and sticks, creating vibrations that travel up and down the length of the rod. The vibrations make sound WAVES.

Sound, like light, travels in waves. When the waves are far apart, the sound has a long WAVELENGTH. When the waves are close together, the sound has a short wavelength.

The wavelength of the sound determines whether you hear a high or low pitch. Short wavelengths are high pitches and long wavelengths are low pitches.

The length of the rod changes the length of the sound waves. As the rod gets longer, the sound waves get longer, too. So, a short rod will make a high-pitch noise and a long rod will make a low-pitch noise.

Playing the singing rod is just like playing the violin. On a violin, the string acts like the rod and the bow is your waxed finger. The harder you press the bow onto the strings, the louder the violin sounds. The singing rod will also get louder when you press your fingers on it harder, and the music it makes will become even more "beautiful."

Perhaps if I used this rod under water, I could communicate with whales and dolphins. Where's my wet suit?

SWIMMING LESSONS

I've never really been able to swim well. I tend to sink. However, I could swim in the right substance if I wanted to.

PROCURE THESE ITEMS

- Clear jar
- Corn syrup or honey
- Water
- Spoon
- Cooking oil
- Rubbing alcohol
- Key, jack, or paper clip
- Raisin, half of a peanut, noodle, piece of cereal, or staple
- Ping-Pong ball or small rubber bouncy ball

DO EXACTLY WHAT IT SAYS HERE

1. Fill the jar one quarter full with the corn syrup or honey.

2. Slowly pour the water onto the back of the spoon and into the jar. The water will float on top of the corn syrup. Fill the jar another one quarter full with water. (Now it's half full.)

3. Repeat step 2, adding the cooking oil and then the rubbing alcohol to the jar.

4. If you don't have four perfectly distinct layers of liquid, go away. Let the jar sit for a bit—the layers will sort themselves out.

5. Carefully and gently drop the items on the list into the jar. Where does each object end up?

DISCOVERING DENSITY

This experiment works because of DENSITY. Density is a measure of how much matter a substance contains, relative to its VOLUME. Less DENSE things float on top of things that are more dense.

Corn syrup is the densest liquid you use, so it sinks to the bottom. Water is less dense, so it floats on top of the corn syrup. Cooking oil is even less dense, so it floats on top of the water. And the alcohol is the least dense, so it floats at the very top. The density and MASS of each object you drop in varies. Where they rest depends on their density.

I won first place at a swim meet in junior high with this experiment. I changed the density of the water in all the lanes. Naturally, I made sure my lane had the density most conducive to quick swimming.

FREAKY NATURE

I whipped up this little beauty for my entry in the Mad Scientist Society's Annual Garden Show. I would have won, too, if only Professor Gomer hadn't brought her giant school bus-eating Venus Flytrap.

PROCURE THESE ITEMS

- White carnation
- Sharp knife
- Two glasses
- Food coloring, two different colors

DO EXACTLY WHAT IT SAYS HERE

1. Carefully split the stem of the carnation with the knife. Don't split it all the way to the bottom of the flower though. Leave at least 4 inches (10.2 cm) of whole stem beneath the blossom.

2. Fill both glasses with water. Add a different color of food coloring to each glass.

3. Place the flower so that one half of the stem is in one glass and the other half of the stem is in the other glass.

4. Wait for a while. (A few hours should do it.)

THE CARNATION EXPLANATION

In my next life, I hope I come back as a liquid. Liquids, particularly water, have some really wacky properties. One of my favorites is how water moves from the glass up through the stem of the carnation and into the tips of the petals.

The carnation (and all plants) has tiny tubes inside it. These tubes are called CAPILLARIES. The water moves up the tubes to the edges of the petals. The food coloring gets sucked up along with the water and dyes the edges of the petals.

You can use a thin coffee stirrer to see this principle in action. Stick it in the glass and watch. The water inside the stirrer will rise higher than the water level in the glass.

Okay, I have to be honest here. This flower is not my invention. Dr. Pete Reedish showed it to me some years ago. He tried to tell me that it grew in an alternate universe where only two colors existed. Ha ha—he's such a joker. The stem is green, so obviously it came from a three-color universe.

PERPETUAL MOTION MACHINE

I burned my candle at both ends inventing this perpetual motion machine!

PROCURE THESE ITEMS

- Table knife
- Candle (the tapered kind)
- Straight pin or needle
- 2 drinking glasses
- 2 saucers
- Matches

DO EXACTLY WHAT IT SAYS HERE

1. Use the table knife to scrape the wax away from the bottom of the candle until you expose the wick on that end.

2. Stick the pin or needle through the middle of the candle.

3. Place the glasses next to each other, slightly farther apart than the width of the candle. Use the pin to balance the candle on the rims of the glasses (see the helpful diagram I drew).

4. Put one saucer underneath each end of the candle. They'll catch the drips of wax.

5. Light both ends of the candle.

THE GRAVITY OF THE SITUATION

The candle will see-saw up and down for hours. As the flame melts the wax, it drips onto the saucer and that end gets lighter. GRAVITY pulls the heavier end down. Then the wax on that end melts faster, making it lighter.

The heat from the flame melts the wax and vaporizes it. (The wax turns into a GAS.) The gas burns instead of the wick.

A perpetual motion machine is a machine that never stops moving. Newton's First Law (the one that says that an object in motion will stay in motion unless acted upon by an outside force) explains how a perpetual motion machine is theoretically possible.

Unfortunately, there are always two outside forces at work on this planet: FRICTION and AIR RESISTANCE. Every time the perpetual motion machine moves, some of its energy is used to counteract friction and air resistance, which means that not all the energy is going into the motion. Over time, friction and air resistance will make the machine stop moving entirely.

Scientists agree that making a perpetual motion machine is actually impossible— unless you rewrite a few fundamental laws of physics or go to outer space. Personally, I'm up for either.

Laboratory Burns to the Ground!

The Mad Scientist's laboratory burned to the ground on Thursday morning. The fire was started by an experiment gone awry. Was he creating a giant heat laser that overloaded? Creating a lightning rod to reanimate Frankenstein?

"Oh no, nothing so exciting as that," the Mad Scientist said. "I left the Perpetual Motion Machine on while I took a bath." He quickly added, "Not that I would tell you if I were working on a giant laser or a reanimation machine. That's none of your business."

The Mad Scientist is looking for a good location for his new laboratory.

ROCKET TO THE MOOOOOON!!!

When I was little, my mother called me a space cadet. Was she making fun of me or letting me know that she really wanted me to be an astronaut when I grew up?

PROCURE THESE ITEMS

- 2-liter plastic bottle
- Scissors
- Cardboard
- Duct tape
- Small nail
- Cork that fits in the neck of the bottle
- Ball-inflating needle
- Water
- Wet suit, raincoat, or bathing suit
- Outdoor area
- Bicycle tire pump

DO EXACTLY WHAT IT SAYS HERE

1. Empty the 2-liter bottle. Cut three triangles from the cardboard. These will be the fins of your rocket. Each one should be about 4 inches (10 cm) long and 3 inches (7.5 cm) wide. Tape the fins to the top of the 2-liter bottle with the duct tape (see the helpful diagram I drew).

2. Use the nail to poke a tiny hole in the cork. The hole should be about the same size as the ball-inflating needle.

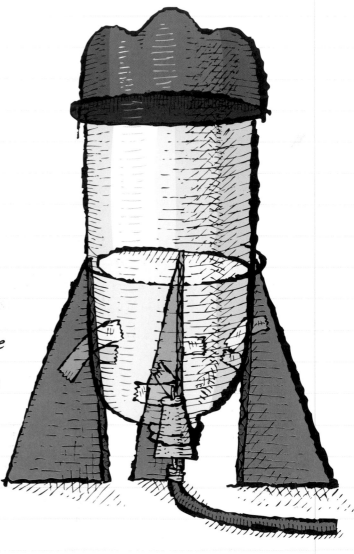

3. Fill the bottle about half full with water. Stick the cork in the bottle. It has to fit snugly. This is your rocket.

4. Put on the wet suit and go outside. Come back inside and get the rocket, the ball-inflating needle, and the bicycle tire pump. Then go outside again.

5. Put the ball-inflating needle in the cork. Set the rocket on a flat surface, resting on its fins.

6. Pump air into the bottle with the bicycle tire pump. Keep pumping until the rocket blasts off.

7. Watch where it lands. Collect the rocket and launch it again. Change the amount of water you put in it. How high can you make the rocket go?

ROCKET SCIENCE

When you pump air into the bottle, the PRESSURE inside the bottle increases. When there's too much air inside the bottle, it has to go somewhere else. The easiest part of the bottle to move is the cork, so the pressure forces the cork out of the neck and the rocket shoots up. That's Newton's Third Law in action (for every action there is an equal and opposite reaction).

If you want your rocket to go even higher, use a smaller bottle. (It has less MASS to move, so it goes higher.)

Now, what are they wearing on the Moon these days?

BURNING METAL

Some people like to burn rubber.
I prefer metal.

PROCURE THESE ITEMS

- Uncoated, extra-course steel wool* (3 x 3 inch [7.6 x 7.6 cm] pad)
- Aluminum pie plate
- Scale
- Tongs
- Lighter

   *If you use fine steel wool, you'll make a sparkler. Pretty, but do this variation outside, well away from important lab notes.

NOTE: Burning metal can be slightly dangerous. Find a gullible adult to hold the tongs and light the steel wool on fire. (For insurance reasons, naturally.)

DO EXACTLY WHAT IT SAYS HERE

1. Put the steel wool on the aluminum pie plate. Weigh them.

2. Hold the steel wool with the tongs. Light it on fire with the lighter.

3. Hold the steel wool over the aluminum plate. Rotate it so that all sides are burned to an even crisp. The steel wool will turn a dull gray color after it's been burned.

4. Collect any pieces that "popped" and flew off. Put them on the plate.

5. Weigh the plate again. Eureka! The steel wool weighs more now!

THE BURNING TRUTH

To burn something, you need fuel and an OXIDANT (oxygen from the air). When you burn the steel wool, you add oxygen from the air to the iron in the wool. (This exact same reaction happens when metal rusts.) When you weigh the steel wool after burning it, the oxygen that's attached itself to the steel wool registers on the scale. That's why the steel wool appears to have gained weight.

This might be a good way to win a wrestling match. I could stuff my wrestling uniform with steel wool and weigh in. Once I'm assigned to a weight class, I burn the steel wool, adding weight to my body. The more weight I have, the larger advantage I'll have over my punier opponents. Brilliant! Now I just need a really good wrestler's name (like The Masked Briquette)...and one of those spandex costumes.

GOOD Uses for Steel Wool

· This experiment
· The Boiling Ice experiment
· Knitting a really strong sweater
· Making a bulletproof sheep

BAD Uses for Steel Wool

· Fireproofing
· Popcorn substitute
· Long underwear
· Pillow stuffing

BOILING ICE

You'd think ice would melt when you boiled it—but you'd be wrong.

PROCURE THESE ITEMS

- Glass test tube
- Crushed ice
- Steel wool
- Cold water
- Metal tongs or test tube holder
- Adult helper
- Candle lighter

DO EXACTLY WHAT IT SAYS HERE

1. Fill the test tube about one-third full with crushed ice. Crushed ice machine not working? Fill a plastic bag with ice and grab a hammer!

2. Pull apart the steel wool pad. Scrunch up a small amount of the steel wool and shove it in the test tube, so it's pressed against the top of the ice. Fill the rest of the test tube with cold water.

3. Hold the test tube with the tongs. Have an adult light the candle lighter and hold it against the part of the test tube where the steel wool is.

4. Boil the water. The ice won't melt!

EUREKA!

Normally ice is less DENSE than water. When water gets warm, it becomes less dense and rises. If you float the ice in the water, the ice will melt because the hot water rising to the top will warm up the ice.

50

However, the steel wool is holding the ice in the bottom of the test tube. The water at the top rises as it heats, so the heat never touches the ice. This process is called CONVECTION.

Could this be a way to save the glaciers from melting? Sink them, cover them with enough tightly packed steel wool to keep them sunk, and then only the surface of the water will heat up. (Polar bears and penguins will need to be fitted with scuba diving equipment.)

Salty Ice Cream

Put 1 tablespoon (15 ml) of sugar, ½ cup (118 ml) of milk, and ¼ teaspoon (1.2 ml) of vanilla in a small plastic bag. Seal the bag. Put this bag inside a larger bag. Fill the larger bag with ice and add 2 tablespoons (30 ml) of rock salt. Seal it. Shake the bag vigorously until the mixture freezes. Then eat the ice cream.

Note: If you don't want to share, get a robot to take a turn shaking the ice cream. (Because robots don't eat ice cream.)

CLOCK REACTION

Time travel is hard on digital watches. I keep the ingredients for this little potion in the trunk of the Time Machine so I can tell time wherever (whenever?) I am.

PROCURE THESE ITEMS

- Measuring cup
- Water
- Small saucepan
- Stove
- Teaspoon
- Cornstarch
- Mixing spoon
- 3 percent hydrogen peroxide
- Medicine dropper
- White vinegar
- Tincture of iodine
- Glass
- Baking powder

DO EXACTLY WHAT IT SAYS HERE

1. Put 1 cup (237 ml) of water in the saucepan. Heat it over medium heat on the stove.

2. Add 1 teaspoon (5 ml) of cornstarch to the water. Stir the mixture until the cornstarch dissolves. Remove the saucepan from the heat.

3. Add 1 cup (237 ml) of water, ½ cup (118 ml) of hydrogen peroxide, and 5 drops of vinegar to the saucepan. Stir them together.

4. Put 2 drops of tincture of iodine in the glass. Then pour the solution from the saucepan into the glass. (You don't have to pour ALL of the solution in. Stop when the glass is full.)

5. Watch the solution turn blue.

6. Add 1 teaspoon (5 ml) of baking powder. Wait a few seconds. The solution will turn clear again.

EUREKA!

If you dump iodine into the cornstarch water, the water will immediately turn blue. That's just what happens when iodine ions react with the cornstarch. But if you put other chemicals in the cornstarch water before adding the iodine, you can slow down the time it takes for the water to turn blue.

When you add hydrogen peroxide and vinegar, they keep the iodine busy for a while. The iodine ions react with the hydrogen peroxide and turn into iodine atoms. Then the iodine atoms react with the vinegar and turn back into iodine ions.

After the iodine is finished reacting with the hydrogen peroxide and vinegar, the iodine can finally react with the cornstarch and turn blue. This is called a clock reaction.

If the world used clock reactions as clocks instead of actual clocks, I could speed up or slow down time whenever I wanted. All I'd need is a never-ending supply of hydrogen peroxide and vinegar.

PETITE PLASTIC

This was my first attempt to create a Shrinking Ray. Unfortunately, it only works on type 6 plastic.

PROCURE THESE ITEMS

- Type 6 plastic items*
- Scissors
- Permanent magic markers
- Oven
- Aluminum foil
- Cookie sheet
- Oven mitt

   *Raid the recycling bin.

DO EXACTLY WHAT IT SAYS HERE

1. Find the recycling symbol on the plastic. Make sure it has a number 6 on it. (Plastic takeout food containers are usually made of number 6 plastic.)

2. Use the scissors to cut a shape out of the plastic. Decorate it with the permanent magic markers.

3. Preheat the oven to 350°F (176.7°C). Put a sheet of aluminum foil, shiny side up, on top of the cookie sheet. Then put the plastic on top of the foil.

4. When the oven is hot, place the cookie sheet in the oven. If you have X-ray glasses or a window in the oven door, watch the plastic shrink. It will curl and wrinkle before it lays flat again. Wait until it lays flat before taking it out of the oven. (Put an oven mitt on first!)

DIMINISHING RETURNS

When the plastic was first made, it was a much thicker and DENSER piece of plastic. Then it went to a plastic food container factory, where it was heated until it was soft and stretched out into the shape of the food container. All the stretching made it quite thin. Then the plastic was cooled very, very quickly. (If it hadn't been cooled quickly, it would have shrunk back into its original shape.) When you put the plastic in the oven and heat it up, it's returning to its original shape and size.

Since this experiment only works on type 6 plastic, it isn't very useful as a functional Shrinking Ray. I wanted to be able to shrink myself. Back to the lab!

PORTABLE AIR CONDITIONER

If there's one thing I hate, it's getting sweat on the Bunsen burner. Until I figure out how to change the tilt of the Earth (or buy that glacier-front laboratory in Alaska), I've got this little trick.

PROCURE THESE ITEMS

- Tablespoon
- Baking soda
- Citric acid*
- Gallon-sized resealable plastic bag
- Sandwich-sized resealable plastic bag
- Water

   *You can find citric acid at the health food store. Don't worry—you don't have to EAT anything from there. Just get the citric acid and get out.

DO EXACTLY WHAT IT SAYS HERE

1. Put 1 tablespoon (15 ml) of baking soda and 1 tablespoon (15 ml) of citric acid in the gallon-sized bag.

2. Fill the sandwich bag about half full with room-temperature water. Don't seal it.

3. Carefully put the sandwich bag inside the gallon-sized bag. Don't spill the water. (Yet.)

4. Seal the gallon-sized bag. Now you spill the water into the bag.

5. Mix the baking soda, citric acid, and water together. Watch the bag inflate. Feel the water. Put on a pair of mittens if your fingers get too cold.

THE FROST FACTOR

The citric acid, baking soda, and water combined to create two new substances: carbon dioxide (the GAS that inflated the bag) and water. The reaction absorbed all the heat from the water, which is why it felt colder. All the heat went into breaking the bonds holding the MOLECULES in the original substances (citric acid and baking soda) together. Whenever heat is used to power a reaction, it's called an ENDOTHERMIC REACTION.

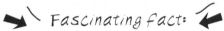
Fascinating fact:
There's actually no such thing as cold—there's just the absence of heat!

When I need to cool off in the summer, I just fill the swimming pool with citric acid and add a dump truck full of baking soda. Sure, I can't swim for a couple of weeks, but at least I can wear my new parka!

PORTABLE HEATER

Sometimes I go a little overboard with the portable air conditioner. I whip this one out when people are getting goosebumps.

PROCURE THESE ITEMS

- Hydrogen peroxide
- Measuring cup
- Plastic bag
- Teaspoon
- Quick-rising dry yeast

DO EXACTLY WHAT IT SAYS HERE

1. Pour ½ cup (59 ml) of hydrogen peroxide into the bag.

2. Add 1 teaspoon (5 ml) of yeast to the bag. Seal the bag.

3. Squish the bag between your fingers to mix the hydrogen peroxide and the yeast together. It will start to bubble and foam.

4. Touch the sides of the bag. Mmmmm...warm!!!

THERMAL THEORY

The hydrogen peroxide reacted chemically with the yeast. It turned into oxygen, water, and heat. (You saw the oxygen escape as a GAS—that's what made the bubbles.) There are many substances that react chemically and release heat just like this. These reactions are called EXOTHERMIC REACTIONS.

One of the fascinating things about exothermic reactions is that they often happen spontaneously. Heh heh heh heh heh.

TRANSPARENT TEA

MY great aunt Matilda has tea at 4 o'clock every day. One time she put so much lemon in her tea, she thought it had disappeared!

PROCURE THESE ITEMS

- Cup
- Boiling water
- Black tea bag
- Lemon
- Cutting board
- Knife
- Baking soda

— NOTE: Don't drink the tea after adding the baking soda. It tastes disgusting, but doesn't make you explode.

DO EXACTLY WHAT IT SAYS HERE

1. Make a cup of tea. (Fill the cup with boiling water and soak the tea bag in it.) Let the tea steep until the water is dark.

2. Cut the lemon into quarters. Squeeze the lemon juice into the tea.

3. Keep adding lemon juice to the tea until the color fades.

4. Add some baking soda to the tea. Keep adding it until the tea darkens again. You can keep doing this for as long as it amuses you.

THE PRINCIPLE OF INVISIBILI-TEA

Black tea is an INDICATOR, like litmus paper. Its color comes from the tannins in the tea. Indicators change color depending on how ACIDIC (or BASIC) a substance is. When you add lemon, it makes the tea acidic, so the color disappears. When you add baking soda, it makes the tea basic, so the color returns.

Does transparent tea stain when you spill it on yourself? I hope not, because this lab coat was brand new.

MY VERY OWN VOLCANO

Sure, a volcano is a good place to hide your secret lab, but imagine how much more useful a portable volcano would be.

NOTE TO SELF:
The mess this experiment made was so gigantic it broke the cleaning robot. Next time, go outside to do this experiment.

PROCURE THESE ITEMS

- 2-liter bottle of diet cola
- Funnel
- Measuring cup
- Rock salt

DO EXACTLY WHAT IT SAYS HERE

1. Place the bottle of cola on the ground outside, away from buildings, open car windows, and pretty much everything that shouldn't have soda on it. Carefully unscrew the cap.

2. Insert the funnel into the top of the bottle.

3. Pour ½ cup (118 ml) of rock salt into the funnel.

4. Run!!!

5. Turn around to watch the awesome eruption.

THE EXPLOSIVE SECRET

The secret behind this explosive reaction lies in the science of fizz. The fizz (called CARBONATION) is caused by carbon dioxide. Carbon dioxide is a GAS that's DISSOLVED in the soda. When you open a new can or bottle of soda, the soda releases the carbon dioxide. It floats to surface, making those little bubbles you see.

Normally, soda releases the carbon dioxide slowly. Eventually, all the carbon dioxide is released and the soda becomes flat. In this experiment, the salt makes the soda let go of the carbon dioxide much faster than it usually does. This creates a lot of PRESSURE, so the soda shoots up and out of the bottle!

At the very least, this soda volcano will create a lot of cavities. Hmmm...perhaps I should look into dentistry.

Things To Do Today
- Develop a plot for world domination
- Re-hide spare key to lab
- Polish Tesla coil
- Research wiener dog/centipede hybrids
- Practice maniacal laughter
- Invent a never-ending chocolate shake
- Rewrite fundamental laws of physics
- Destroy plans for Ice Cream-Eating Robot
- Pick up Radiation Suit from cleaners
- Stock up on cornstarch, salt, and depleted uranium
- Train extra-feral Guard Potato
- Get sized for spandex suit
- Bioengineer a Venus Flytrap that will eat a schoolbus-eating Venus Flytrap

DISAPPEARING TEST TUBE

This experiment is as close to making something invisible as I've ever come.

PROCURE THESE ITEMS

- Pyrex test tube
- Glass jar (a spaghetti-sauce or pickle jar is about the right size)
- Vegetable oil*

   *Wesson cooking oil works best.

DO EXACTLY WHAT IT SAYS HERE

1. Carefully examine both the test tube and the glass jar carefully. While they are both technically "see-through," you can see them. (If you can't, you might want to get your eyes checked.)

2. Put the test tube inside the jar.

3. Fill the jar and the test tube with vegetable oil.

4. Look for the test tube.

INVISIBILITY EXPLAINED

When light passes through anything more DENSE than air, it slows down and bends. How much the light bends is called the INDEX OF REFRACTION.

Scientists calculate a material's index of refraction by dividing the speed of light in a VACUUM by the speed of light as it travels through the material. (I left my light-speed measuring tape in my other lab coat, so you'll just have to trust me on this one.)

The test tube disappears because its index of refraction matches the oil's index of refraction. If an object (such as a pyrex test tube) is submerged in a liquid that has the exact same index of refraction (such as cooking oil), the light doesn't slow down or bend as it travels from one material to the next. This makes the object disappear!

In general, the denser a material is, the higher its index of refraction will be. The higher the index of refraction, the more light bends. A diamond has a very high index of refraction. That's what makes diamonds sparkle.

So, if I find a liquid that has the exact same index of refraction as a diamond, I can walk into a jewelry store, put all the diamonds in my liquid, and walk right out without anyone knowing!

PLASTIC MILK

The best thing about being a Mad Scientist:
Nobody can tell you not to play with your food!

PROCURE THESE ITEMS

- Measuring cup
- Skim milk (from a cow, not a soybean or a goat)
- Microwaveable bowl
- Teaspoon
- White vinegar
- Microwave
- Mixing spoon
- Sieve
- Sink

DO EXACTLY WHAT IT SAYS HERE

1. Pour 1½ cups (355 ml) of skim milk in the bowl. Add 4 teaspoons (19.7 ml) of vinegar.

2. Microwave the concoction on high for one minute. It will separate into a liquid and a solid.

3. Stir the concoction. Then pour it through the sieve into the sink. The liquid will go down the drain. That's not the part you want anyway.

4. The good stuff is in the sieve. Let it cool and lightly rinse it off.

5. Play with the gooey stuff. Mold it. Shape it. Pull it slowly and watch it stretch. Pull it quickly to tear it.

NOTE: Don't put the gooey stuff down the drain. Store it in an airtight plastic container until you're done with it. Then put it in the trash.

THE SECRET CONGEALED

If I were a chef (and I almost was), I would say that the milk curdled. And I'd probably be very unhappy about it. Luckily, as a scientist I can celebrate this brand new concoction! It's a POLYMER, and I have a particularly soft spot in my heart for polymers.

Polymers are made up of long chains of MOLECULES. (The most common polymers are plastics.) You can stretch the polymer slowly forever—the long chains just keep stretching out. But if you tug hard, you can pull the chains apart.

This milk-based polymer was created by an acid/base reaction. The vinegar is an ACID. The milk is a BASE. When acids and bases mix, both change. In this particular reaction the base (milk) separates into casein (a protein) and whey. The vinegar turns the casein into a solid. The whey becomes a much thinner liquid. (You poured the whey down the drain.) The vinegar reacted with the casein proteins, causing them to form long chains of molecules—a polymer!

Sometimes I fall asleep reciting all the polymers I can think of: paper, rubber, CDs, computers, shampoo, play dough, straws, hair spray, tooth-brushes, chewing gum, bulletproof vests, bicycle tires, fireproof clothing, styrofoam cups, frisbees, cell phones, parachutes, pantyhose, ladders, musical instruments, diapers, my teddy bear

BENDABLE BONES

Have you ever heard of
boneless chicken?
This is the next best thing.

PROCURE THESE ITEMS

- Clean chicken bones
- Large jar
- White vinegar

DO EXACTLY WHAT IT SAYS HERE

1. Put the chicken bones in the jar.

2. Pour vinegar into the jar. Use enough to cover the bones completely.

3. Set the jar on the counter and leave it alone for three days.

4. At the end of three days (no cheating!), come back and take the bones out of the jar.

5. Bend the bones. Can you tie them in knots? If not, stick them back in the jar, replace the vinegar, and wait four more days before trying it again. (Hey, nobody said science was easy.)

FLEXIBLE FUN!

Bones contain two important MINERALS, calcium and phosphorus. These minerals make bones hard and stiff. (And capable of holding you together.) The acetic acid in the vinegar reacts with the minerals, DISSOLVING them. All that's left of the bone is the flexible cartilage, which is why you can bend them.

Now, if I soaked my bones in vinegar, I could finally win a limbo contest. And I could sneak into places through the air ducts to steal stuff. Pardon me while I go fill my bathtub with vinegar...

INVISIBLE INKS

I was going to write this entire notebook in invisible ink, but if the power went out, how would I be able to read it?

CHEMISTRY INVISIBLE INK

Don't let the name of this ink fool you! You don't need a Bunsen burner or an Erlenmeyer flask to make it.

PROCURE THESE ITEMS

- Tablespoon
- Baking soda
- Water
- Cup
- Small paintbrush
- White paper
- Lightbulb or oven

DO EXACTLY WHAT IT SAYS HERE

1. Mix 1 tablespoon (15 ml) of baking soda with 1 tablespoon (15 ml) of water in a cup. (If you want to make enough ink to write a manifesto, just mix equal parts baking soda and water.)

2. Use the paintbrush to write your message on a piece of paper. Let the message dry completely.

3. To reveal the writing, hold the paper over a lightbulb (turn the lightbulb on first) or put it on a cookie sheet in a 300°F (149°C) oven for 10 minutes.

STINKY INK

Wear your lab goggles so you don't end up crying over this concoction.

PROCURE THESE ITEMS

- Lab goggles
- Grater
- Onion
- Saucer
- Tea strainer
- Spoon
- Clean jar
- Paintbrush or toothpick
- Paper

DO EXACTLY WHAT IT SAYS HERE

1. Put on your lab goggles.
   (Unless you're so evil, even onions can't make you cry.)

2. Grate the onion onto the saucer. Scoop it into the strainer.

3. Press the back of the spoon against the onion goop. Squeeze the juice through the strainer and into the jar.

4. Dip the brush into the jar. Use the onion juice as ink. Write your message on the paper. Let the writing dry.

5. To reveal the writing, hold the paper over a lightbulb (turn the lightbulb on first) or put it on a cookie sheet in a 300°F (149°C) oven for 10 minutes.

FRUIT INK

If you don't mind draining power from your lemon juice light, you can use it to make invisible ink.

PROCURE THESE ITEMS

- Paper clip or toothpick
- Lemon, apple, grapefruit, or orange
- Paper

DO EXACTLY WHAT IT SAYS HERE

1. Unbend the paper clip. Stick the end into the fruit. Make sure you get below the skin. Coat the tip of the paper clip with juice.

2. Write on the paper with the juice ink. Let the writing dry.

3. To reveal the writing, hold the paper over a lightbulb (turn the lightbulb on first) or put it on a cookie sheet in a 300°F (149°C) oven for 10 minutes.

HOW INVISIBLE INKS WORK

All of these inks are heat-activated—when you warm them up, the message appears. Paper burns at 451°F (233°C). These inks lower the temperature at which paper burns (called the FLASH POINT). That means the paper that has the ink on it will char (burn) at a lower temperature than the rest of the paper.

I made a map of my secret underground fortress with this ink. Now if only I could figure out which one of these pieces of blank paper I drew that on...

MAGNETIC FLUID

You don't need superpowers to control metal—just a magnet and some vegetable oil.

PROCURE THESE ITEMS

- Dry sand from the beach*
- Paper plates
- Strong magnet
- Plastic bag
- Small plastic or paper cups
- Vegetable oil
- Plastic spoon or wooden popsicle stick

*You can buy iron filings from science supply stores if you don't want to mine them from the sand. Skip step 1.

DO EXACTLY WHAT IT SAYS HERE

1. Spread the sand on the paper plate. Make sure the sand is dry. Put the magnet in the plastic bag. Hold the magnet over the sand. Iron filings will jump from the sand onto the magnet. Put the filings you mined on the second plate. Do this until you have mined a handful of iron filings.

2. Pour the iron filings into the cup. They should fill about a third of the cup. Pour a little bit of vegetable oil into the cup. Stir it with the plastic spoon or popsicle stick.

3. Keep adding vegetable oil, a little bit at a time, and keep stirring the mixture until you have a thin black paste.

4. Hold the magnet against the side of the cup. The filings will stiffen against the side of the cup where the magnet is. Let go of the magnet. The filings will hold the magnet in place.

5. Leave the magnet where it is. Then, tip the cup over, pouring the excess vegetable oil into another cup. If a few filings pour out of the cup, too, don't worry about it.

6. Stand the cup upright again and remove the magnet. Use the spoon to stir the mixture. The longer you stir, the easier it is to do.

7. Tip the cup to one side and stick the spoon in the liquid. Put the magnet on the bottom of the cup. Let go of the spoon. What happens?

8. Remove the magnet and stir the mixture until it becomes liquid again. Then pour it into the plastic bag. Stick a magnet to the outside. You can manipulate the hardened mixture like clay. When you take away the magnet, it will turn into a puddle.

NOTE: When you're tired of this stuff, you can wash it down the drain with lots and lots of water.

THE MYSTERIES OF MAGNETISM

The iron filings are attracted to the magnet. If you stick the magnet in the pile of iron filings, it'll stick to the magnet and will be impossible to get off. And oil just sits in a puddle most of the time. But when you mix the two together and then put a magnetic field next to them, the mixture hardens. The iron filings form a lattice shape that feels more solid than a puddle of oil or the iron by itself.

I'm going to use a magnetic fluid to make a ladder to the loft in my lab. (I keep all the top-secret experiments in the loft.) After I climb up the ladder, all I have to do is take away the magnets and the ladder will collapse. No one else will be able to get up there. Of course, if all the iron filings are in a puddle on the floor and I'm stuck in the loft, rebuilding the magnetic ladder may be a bit problematic...

MUMMY BOTANY

Biology is the study of living things, but you usually study them once they're dead. When the (formerly) living things you're studying are plants, it's called botany. Anyway, I made these flowers for my mummy.

PROCURE THESE ITEMS

- Measuring cup
- Borax*
- Cornstarch
- Container with a snap-fit lid
- Flowers
- Soft-bristled paintbrush
- Newspaper and acrylic spray sealant (optional)

   *You can find borax on the laundry aisle at the grocery store.

DO EXACTLY WHAT IT SAYS HERE

1. Put ½ cup (118 ml) of borax and 1 cup (237 ml) of cornstarch in the bottom of the container. Put the lid on and shake it up.

2. Place the first flower in the container. Gently cover it with the mixture. If the flower has lots of overlapping petals, sprinkle the mixture between the petals before putting the flower in the container.

3. Put as many flowers as you want in the container. Then snap on the lid.

4. Store the container at room temperature for seven to 10 days. Do not open the container before that. (If you get impatient, work on your Time Machine. This is one of those situations in which it would be useful.)

5. Open the container, then pour off the mixture. Use the paintbrush to dust off the petals.

6. If you're planning on keeping your dried flowers for ever and ever and ever, place them on top of the newspaper and spray them with the acrylic spray sealant.

THE DELIGHTS OF DESICCATION

The water in the CELLS of organic matter, such as flowers, provides a very fertile feeding ground for bacteria and mold. Bacteria and mold DECOMPOSE the cells, leading to rot and decay.

To prevent rot and decay, all you have to do is suck out all the water. (This process is called DESICCATION.) Borax and cornstarch are both HYGROSCOPIC, which means they absorb water. When you cover the flower with a hygroscopic substance, all the water gets sucked out of it. Then there's no food for bacteria and mold to grow on and the flower is preserved.

If you want the desiccated flowers to last forever, you have to protect them from the moisture in the air. The acrylic spray sealant coats the flowers with acrylic, protecting them from moisture. Now your daisies will never be pushing up daisies!

Mummies are made with this exact same process (but slightly different chemicals). I used up all my dead bodies testing out the Reanimation Machine, so I picked flowers from my neighbors' garden for this experiment. I don't think they've noticed their flowers are missing yet.

THE OLD PLANT TRICK

I stayed awake late last night wondering if plants have some sort of magical ability to tell up from down.

PROCURE THESE ITEMS

- Gelatin dessert mix
- Clear plastic cups
- Radish seeds
- Toothpick
- Plastic wrap
- Rubber band

NOTE: A lot of things will grow in gelatin, not just radishes. Bacteria are particularly fond of it. Throw out your gelatin when you've completed this experiment.

DO EXACTLY WHAT IT SAYS HERE

1. Make the gelatin dessert according to the directions on the package. Pour it into a cup and let it set.

2. When the gelatin is firm, sprinkle a few radish seeds on the surface. Use the toothpick to gently push the seeds about 1/8 inch (3 mm) below the surface of the gelatin.

3. Place the gelatin away from direct sunlight, but don't put it in the fridge! The seeds will need light to grow, but if sunlight hits the gelatin, it may melt.

4. Check on your experiment every day. You'll see the seeds sprout.

5. Once the roots of the radishes are about 1 inch (2.5 cm) long, cover the top of the cup with the plastic wrap. Poke holes in it so that the

stems and leaves can get through. Use the rubber band to hold the plastic wrap tightly on the cup.

6. Turn the cup upside down. The plastic wrap should hold the gelatin in place.

7. Balance the lip of the cup between two more cups so that it's held upside down. What happens to the roots as the plants continue to grow?

EUREKA!

When the plant was flipped upside down, the roots started growing the opposite way. How do plants know which way is up? They can detect GRAVITY. This is called GRAVITROPISM. Plants have DENSE materials in their CELLS called amyloplasts. The amyloplasts are heavier than anything else inside the cell. Gravity pulls them down, so the seeds know which way to grow.

I don't always know which way is down. Once, I got flipped upside down in the hot air balloon hang glider I invented. I thought I was right side up—I mean, the clouds were above me—until I almost collided with an upside-down airplane. Maybe I should inject myself with amyloplasts.

HOVERCRAFT

This is one of my favorite ways to get around. It's not like I'm going to take a taxi to the laboratory.

PROCURE THESE ITEMS

- Small plastic spool
- CD
- Super strong glue
- Balloon
- Twist tie (optional)
- Table
- Bendable drinking straw (optional)

DO EXACTLY WHAT IT SAYS HERE

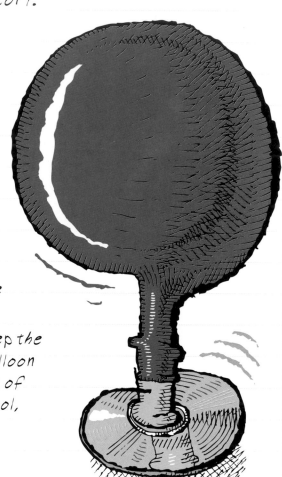

1. Put the spool on top of the CD. Line up the hole in the middle of the spool with the one in the CD. Glue it in place. Let the glue dry.

2. Blow up the balloon. Pinch the neck to keep the air in, and then stretch the lip of the balloon around the top of the spool. If the neck of the balloon is too large to fit on the spool, use the twist tie to hold it in place.

3. Put the CD on the table and let go of the balloon.

4. If you'd like to be able to steer your hovercraft (which is sometimes useful), slip the bendable end of the drinking straw between the lip of the balloon and the spool. Rotate the drinking straw to steer.

THE SCIENTIFIC SECRET REVEALED

When the CD is just sitting on the table (or anywhere else), the contact between the bottom of the CD and the top of the table creates FRICTION. Friction is a force between two objects that resists movement. It takes energy to overcome the awesome powers of friction. Sometimes it's easier just to eliminate some of the friction.

The hovercraft works by getting rid of the friction between the CD and the table. When the air squeezes out of the balloon, it moves through the spool and beneath the CD. The air creates a cushion between the bottom of the CD and the table. There's a lot less friction between the air and the CD than there is between the CD and the table, so the hovercraft slides along on this cushion.

Now, as soon as I invent a working Shrinking Ray, I can take the hovercraft out for a spin.

OTHER POSSIBLE METHODS OF TRANSPORTATION

➡ Build a gigantic catapult (investigate appropriate landing gear)

➡ Invent a device that creates holes in Space-Time Continuum

➡ Flood the planet with the Tsunami Machine and use a raft

➡ Jet pack (figure out how to steer it)

➡ Find hot air balloon hang glider (maybe it's in the basement?)

➡ Glue huge springs to the bottom of my shoes

➡ Ride the giant chicken

GLOSSARY

(These are just a few of my favorite words.)

ACID. A compound that reacts with a base to form salt.

ACIDIC. A substance that contains a lot of acid.

AIR RESISTANCE. The force of air which opposes motion.

BASE. A compound that reacts with an acid to form salt.

BASIC. A substance that contains a lot of base. (Not the rock-and-roll kind.)

CAPILLARIES. Tiny tubes that move liquid through tissue.

CARBONATION. The process of putting carbon dioxide into a liquid so that it becomes bubbly and gaseous.

CELL. In biology, a cell is one of the basic building blocks of matter. In electricity, a cell is a unit that turns energy into electricity. (It's best not to confuse the two.)

CENTER OF GRAVITY. The point around which an object's weight is evenly distributed.

COLLOID. A substance that acts like both a liquid and a solid.

CONDENSE. When a gas turns into a liquid.

CONDUCTOR. A substance that lets electricity, heat, light, or sound move through it.

CONVECTION. One of the ways heat travels.

DECOMPOSE. When something breaks down into its simpler elements.

DENSE. The amount of mass an object has, relative to its volume.

DENSITY. The measurement of how dense an object is.

DEOXYRIBONUCLEIC ACID. The molecule that contains genetic information that will determine how the cells grow and develop.

DESICCATION. The process of removing all moisture from something.

DISSOLVE. To become part of a solution.

DNA. Deoxyribonucleic acid. Aren't you glad you asked? (See above.)

ELECTRON. The particle of an atom that has a negative electrical charge.

ELECTRORHEOLOGICAL. A fluid that reacts to an electrical field by changing viscosity.

ENDOTHERMIC REACTION. A reaction that absorbs heat.

ENZYMES. The proteins that living cells make in order to digest stuff.

EVAPORATE. To change from a liquid to a gas.

EXOTHERMIC REACTION. A reaction that gives off heat.

FLASH POINT. The precise temperature at which a substance burns.

FRICTION. The force that resists movement when two things are in contact.

GAS. A substance like air that is neither a liquid nor a solid at ordinary temperatures and that has the ability to expand indefinitely.

GRAVITROPISM. An organism's response to gravity, such as a plant figuring out which way is down.

GRAVITY. The force that keeps me in bed at night. And pulls on everything else equally.

HELIOTROPIC. An organism that grows toward or away from the sun.

HYGROSCOPIC. A substance that loves water so much, it will suck it out of anything it comes in contact with. (Sort of like a vampire, but it only drinks water.)

INDEX OF REFRACTION. The measurement of how much light slows and bends when it moves through an object.

INDICATOR. A chemical that changes color when exposed to different substances.

INERTIA. The tendency of an object to keep moving if it is already moving and to stay still if it is already still.

MASS. The measurement of the amount of matter something has.

MELTING POINT. The temperature at which a solid turns into a liquid.

MEMBRANE. A thin, flexible layer that liquids can pass through.

MINERAL. A solid, inorganic substance that has a specific crystal structure. (Diamonds are my favorite mineral.)

MOLECULE. The smallest physical unit of a compound, consisting of one or more atoms held together by chemical bonds.

NUCLEUS. The core of a cell (the biological kind) or atom.

OSMOSIS. The spontaneous movement of a liquid through a membrane.

OXIDANT. Something that adds oxygen to a substance.

PHOTOSYNTHESIS. The process by which plants turn sunlight into food (for them, not necessarily for us).

POLYMER. A natural or artificial compound made of long chains of identical molecules.

PRESSURE. Continuous force applied by one thing to another.

SATURATED SOLUTION. A solution in which no more solute can be dissolved.

SOLUTE. A substance that dissolves in a solvent to create a solution.

SOLUTION. The answer to a problem. Or, more often, a material made up of two or more substances mixed together uniformly. (Remember: a solution isn't always the solution to the problem at hand.)

SOLVENT. A substance that dissolves a solute to create a solution.

VACUUM. Emptiness caused by the removal of all gases.

VISCOSITY. A substance's resistance to flow.

VOLTAIC PILE. A cell that creates electricity through a chemical reaction.

VOLUME. The amount of space something takes up.

WAVE. One of the many ways different forms of energy can move. (Think about the waves on the ocean. That's a wave.)

WAVELENGTH. The distance between the peaks of one wave and the next. (This is how you know how big a wave is.)

ACKNOWLEDGMENTS

This book would not have been possible without the hard work and awesome talents of the following people:

Celia Naranjo, who imagined what this book would look like and then made it happen.

Gina Barrier, the chemistry whiz who made sure no drastic lab accidents would occur when performing these experiments.

Rachel Nagy, who shared her table so Ian could draw, draw, and draw some more.

Diane Kisselberg, who made sure we spelled words like "electrorheological" correctly.

Erik Johnson, who came through with bad puns in the nick of time.

I was so pleased with your contributions that I'd like to invite each and every one of you to become my lab assistant!

I've just finished the prototype of my teleportation machine... Who wants to go first?

—THE MAD SCIENTIST

INDEX